Subconscious Discussions

Ashley Dhillon

Presentation by *BookLeaf Publishing*

Web: www.bookleafpub.com

E-mail: info@bookleafpub.com

ISBN: 9789357690867

First edition 2022

ONE

1

If you feel as though you are stuck
In a perpetual winter

Remember,
Even after losing its leaves,
Its identity and beauty.
After being stripped bare and exposed to the
core,

Spring will return and balance will be restored,
And the tree will be mighty once again.

Hope will always come back and bloom.

TWO

I see your hands and its torture.

I long to hold them, feel them on my skin
Opening my buttons, my heart, my secrets
within.

There's electricity when we touch, I know you
feel it too;
My queen is exposed, waiting for you to make a
move.

If only you knew the power you have,
Its all up to you, its all in your hands.

THREE

3

How terrifying and freeing to let someone in,
To let them see in behind the walls.
The ones you've built to protect yourself,
In case you should ever fall.

But that can be a lonely life,
Never letting your true self show.
Bonds you have will be stuck on the surface,
Without any chance to grow.

So break those imaginary walls down
And allow yourself to truly shine.
By opening up, your life will too,
In only a matter of time.

FOUR

We live in a world in which even when
surrounded by others,
It is only white noise.
It is empty, meaningless chatter
That only barely scratches the surface.

Yet, when alone, the silence is deafening.
Our thoughts come to life.
The anxieties and fears speaking the loudest,
until they block out all else.

Maybe with a little compassion for one another
We can break this cycle.

FIVE

My tears are my strength.

They are an insight into my soul.
A subtle demonstration
Of just how deeply I feel.

Each tear tells a story of its own,
A unique representation
Of a little piece of my heart.

Do not mistake them for weakness.
With each one that falls,
I only grow stronger.

SIX

There is so much pressure in today's society,
Without any context, you have all these plans for
me.

According to you I should be a mother and a
wife,
But let me kindly remind you that this is my life.

Please don't tell me I am next or out of time,
Last time I checked, I am doing just fine.

Instead of judging me for all the things that I am
not,
Maybe you could ask me what I really want.

So forgive me but I will not blindly conform,
Just because it is your idea of the social norm.

SEVEN

As the temperature cools,
The colours get warmer.
Even the leaves
Impress us
With their glowing hues.

I always long for the time of year
When the days get shorter
And the lights are on display.
The moon even shines brighter.
There is an element of excitement
With the crisp air.

It is nature's coming of age,
There is beauty everywhere you go.
My favourite season.

EIGHT

What are you?
Not always asked with negative intent,
But still a demeaning question.

It has become normal to focus
On the differences between us
As a means for separation rather than
Coming together
To celebrate them.

Asking me what I am
It insinuates that I am a thing,
An object,
Incapable of feeling and thinking.

Yes, I may look different
But I am still a person,
An emotional being.

Why is it important what I am?
When we leave this life, on our tombstones
Our lives will be represented by a single line;
Our ashes will burn to the same colour.
So what difference does it make?

What's on the outside is irrelevant,
It does not make my character.
On the inside, I am made up the same as you.

As for an answer, it is this,
I am human.
Just like you, just like the next person,
And quite frankly,
I don't owe you anything more than that.

NINE

Have you ever seen a person
And just have always known,
That from that moment onwards
You will never be alone.

That you share an instant connection,
Puzzle pieces perfectly aligned,
Who seem to have that magic
So many people search to find.

Even if the timing is not quite right
There isn't ever any doubt.
When it is meant to be,
Two souls will seek each other out.

So be patient and look for the signs
And always follow your heart.
True love is out there waiting,
You'll recognize it right at the start.

TEN

If what you fear
Is the unknown,
Don't.

Embrace it. Run to it.
Make the leap, take the risk.
You owe this to yourself.

Even if you fail, it is better
Than being haunted by
What if.

ELEVEN

Grief
It works in mysterious ways.
Sometimes it is a tidal wave
Of emotions so strong,
You are drowning in them
From the very moment you wake up.
Making something as simple
As getting out of bed
Seem impossible.

At other times
It is a constant dull ache.
Not enough to stop you,
But just the right amount
To always remind you of your pain.

Yet at moments
There can be a reprieve
And the sun breaks through the clouds.
For a brief moment,
Everything is okay,
Before the overwhelming feeling returns.

But this is the price we pay,
For being human,
For having a heart, the capacity to love,
Which is better than not feeling at all.

TWELVE

You must think I'm stupid, maybe that is true
Because I trusted you and got played the fool.

For far too long, I gave you the benefit of the
doubt,
But you didn't think twice when selling me out.

I don't understand though, why all the games,
Because for you there was nothing to gain.

My name was dragged through the mud due to
your lies
You tried to take me down with you in your own
demise.

Now you've cried wolf one too many times,
Looking back I wish I had seen the signs.

One day, if its the last thing I do,
I will show the truth and expose the real you.

THIRTEEN

15

Written words
Carry magic within them.

They paint the picture,
But you get to decide
What colours to use.

They are merely words on a page
Until you
Bring them to life.

FOURTEEN

It was never my intent.

I let my fears take hold;
My doubts and insecurities
Hid the true me.
The one I wanted you to see.

It's ironic,
By hiding myself, I hid you too.
Someone I truly wanted to hold,
Only could remain
Just out of reach.

I am so sorry
For not being able,
To see you,
The way you deserved.
As I sit here,
Looking at these fingers,
That let something great slip right through.

FIFTEEN

To everyone else I look just fine,
But they can't see into my brain.
Although it may hurt physically,
Nothing compares to the mental pain.

But I had support right from the start,
Even when I thought I had to fight on my own.
The magnitude is overwhelming
When you realize you are not alone.

By sitting next to me in the dark
And simply lending an ear
You helped me stay afloat,
Despite the fact I was drowning in fear.

I am not defined by my struggles,
But rather on how I choose to persevere,
Which would have been impossible without you,
Your belief in me got me here.

SIXTEEN

Why is it so easy?
To give the best of me,
Show patience and understanding
To everyone,
Except the one I see everyday
Looking back at me
In the mirror.

To her I am the most critical;
All I see are her flaws.
It seems impossible
For her to do anything right.
She has never seemed worthy,
She has never been enough
And will never live up to expectations.

Though outside of the mirror,
I choose to see the good in others,
Forgiveness is always an option.
I only hope one day,
I can learn to see my reflection
Through the same lens
I use to see everybody else.

S E V E N T E E N

"I'm sorry you're too young to understand"

I will not let that define me, I am more than just
my age,
So keep your attempted apology, it only fills me
with more rage.

Worldly experience doesn't mean more trips
around the sun,
You have no idea about all the things I've
overcome.

I may see things differently, but it doesn't mean
I'm wrong,
Maybe you've been stuck in your ways for too
long.

So don't try to silence me and my point of view,
It probably hurts because you know its true.

I'm sorry you're too stubborn that you will
NEVER understand,
The pain you caused
With the judgements you made,
The lines you drew

With the games you played,
All could have been avoided if you'd only lent a
hand.

EIGHTEEN

21

A true friend
Although sometimes hard to come by,
Is one of the greatest gifts.

It is the most freeing feeling,
Allowing you to be the truest version of
yourself.

You never question if they will be there for you.
Joy, heartbreak, disappointment,
It makes no difference.

They hold you accountable
Without ever passing judgement.
They dig deep and see the real you,
Never requiring an explanation.

When you have this
The word friend is inadequate.
You have found family.

NINETEEN

I still sometimes wonder if this will ever feel
real,
Just saying I miss you doesn't encompass how I
feel.

From the moment you left us, life has never
been the same,
It can all come flooding back with the mention
of your name.

You were the glue that kept us all together
I still can't comprehend that you are gone
forever.

But I can still feel you with me every single day
And I'm starting to realize you haven't gone
away.

My first friend, my person, right from the start,
Which is a bond I'll always carry within my
heart.

Even though it hurts and you were gone far too
soon,
I am grateful to have known someone like you.

Our memories and stories are an integral piece
of me
You have left behind a lasting legacy.

I will never stop trying to make you proud,
Because I know you're watching from among the
clouds.

9 789335 769086 7